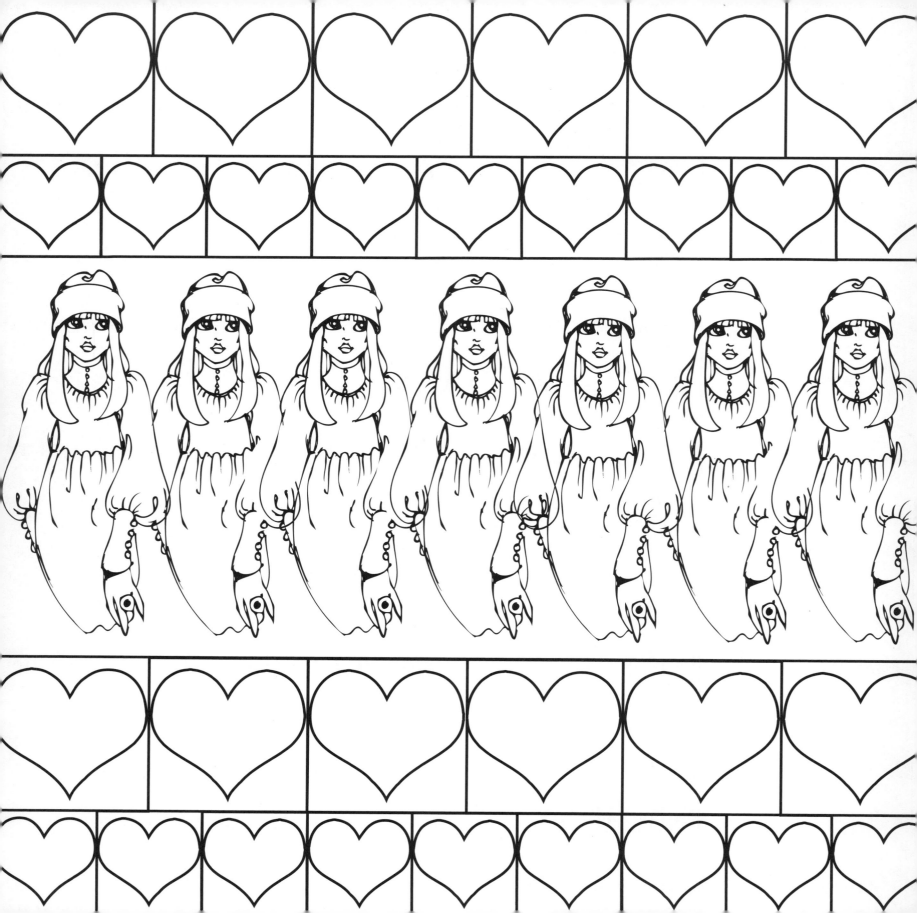

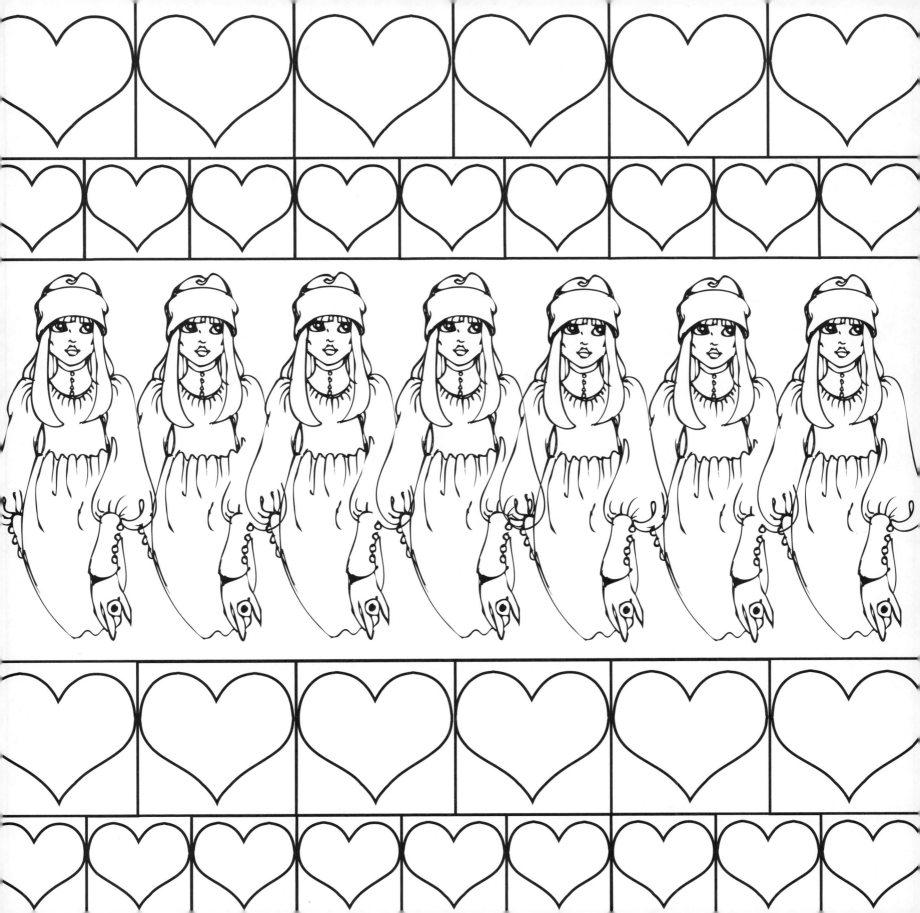

# EYES & MAKEUP

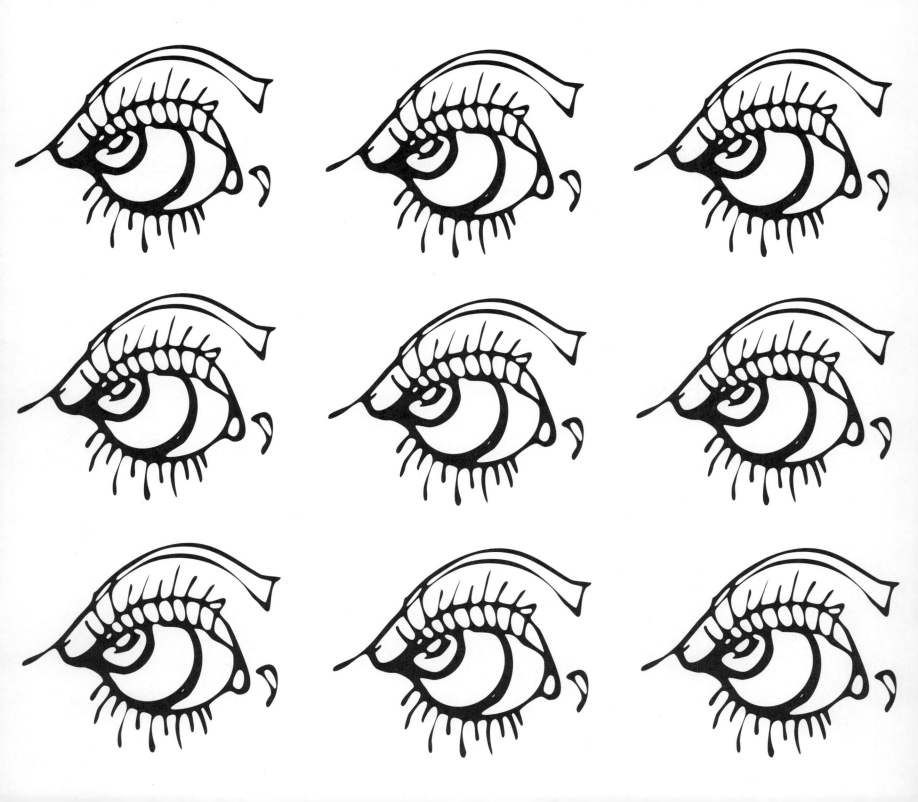

# EYES & MAKEUP

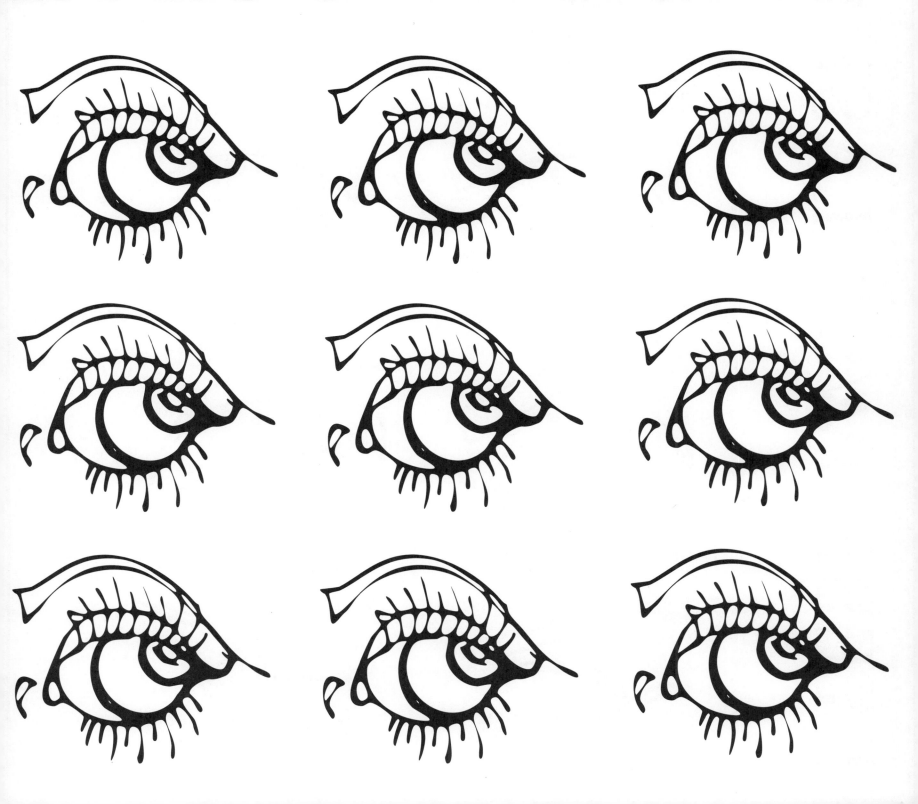

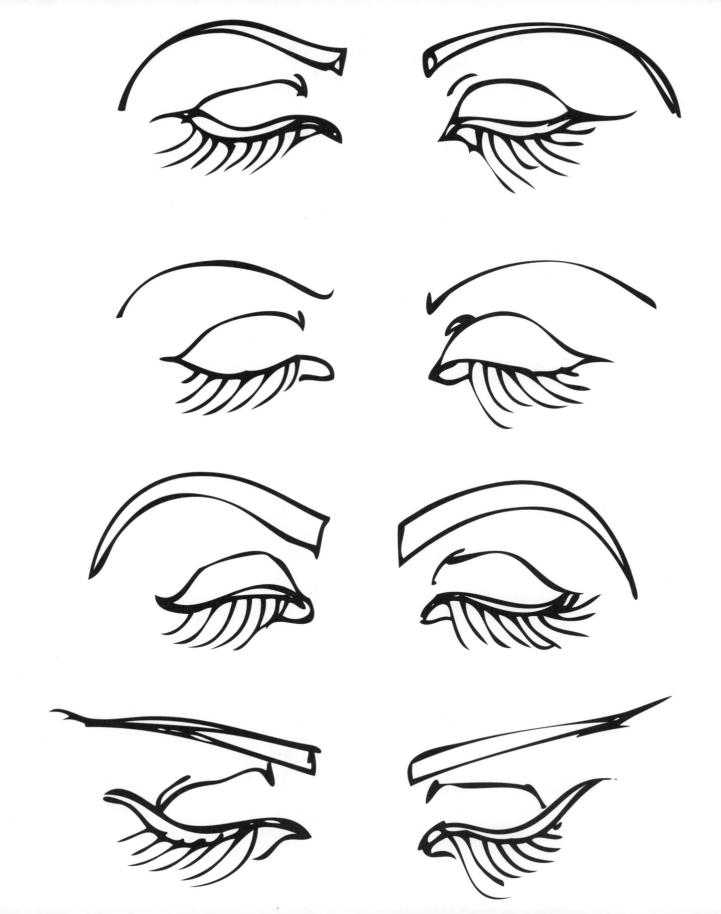

EYEBROWS & LASHES

EYEBROWS & LASHES

# LIPS & LIPSTICK

# LIPSTICK & LIPS

# HAIR & HATS

# HAIR & HATS

# HAT & MAKEUP

# HAT & MAKEUP

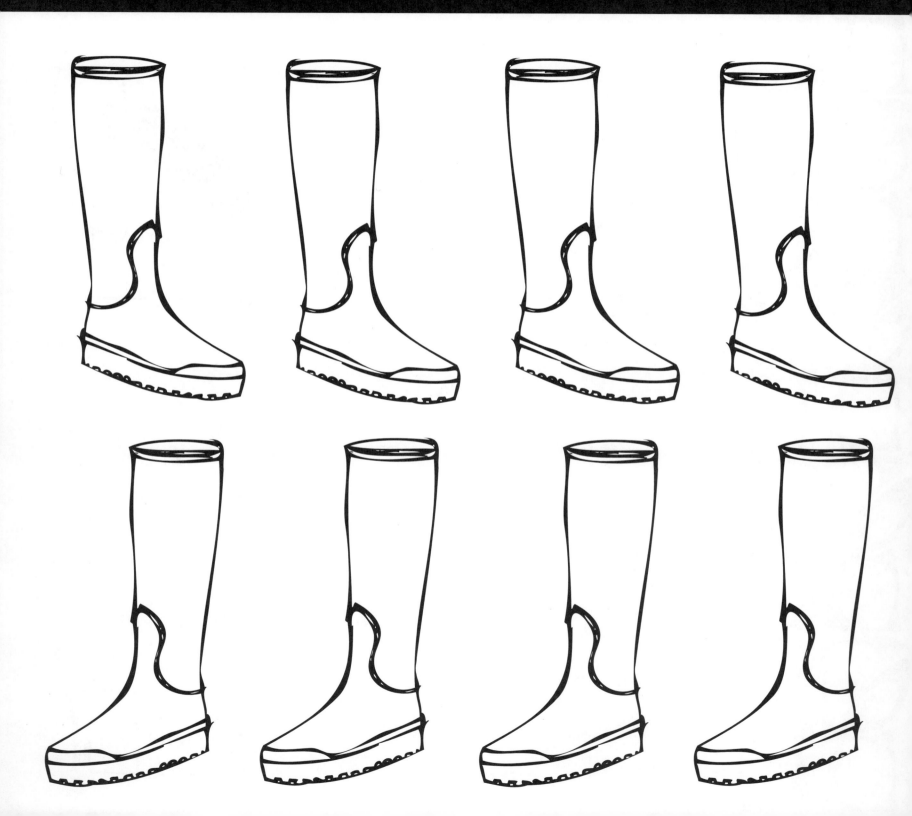

# WELLINGTON BOOTS

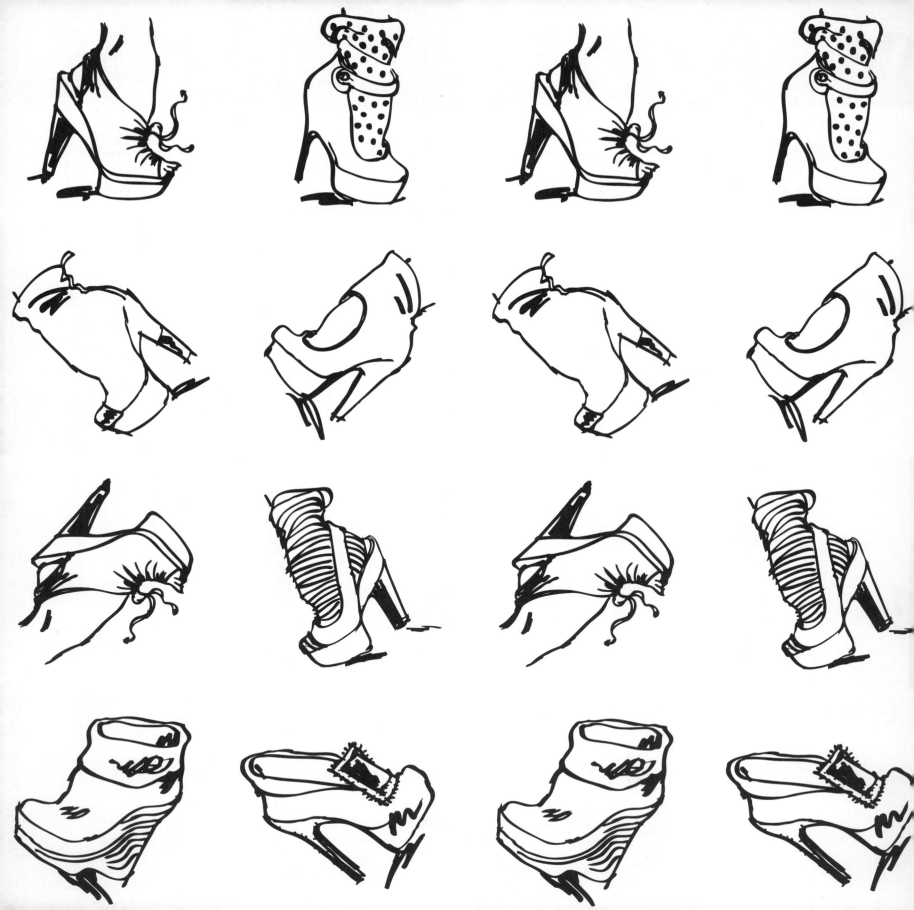

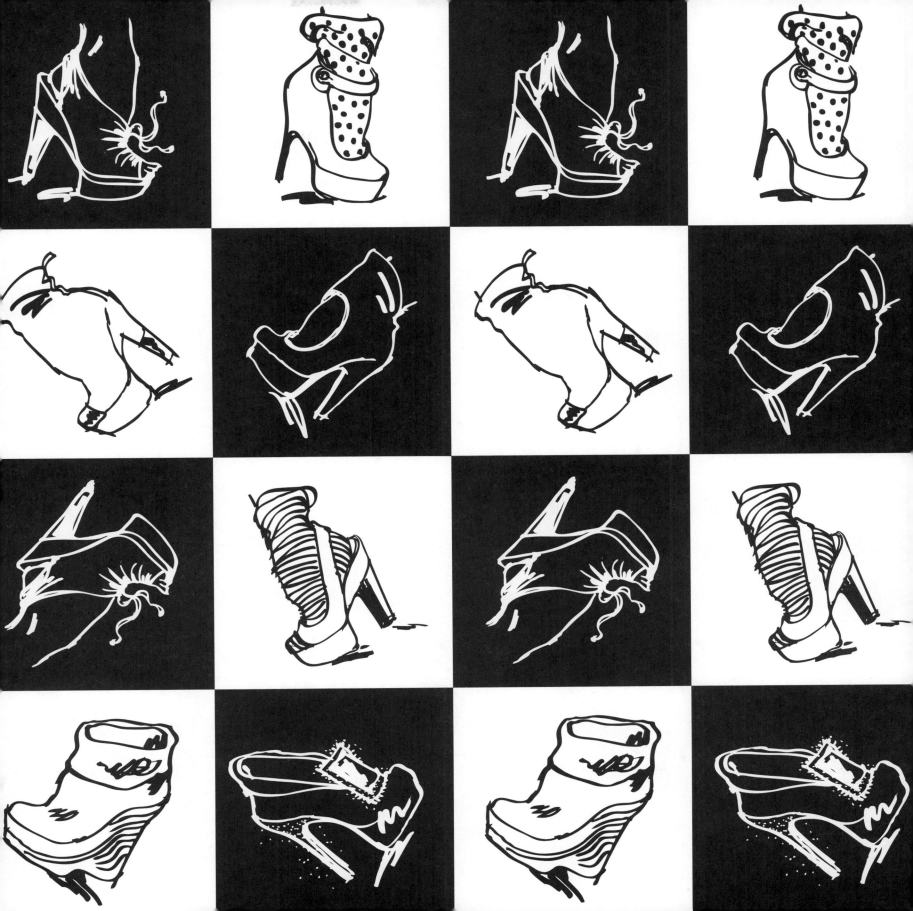

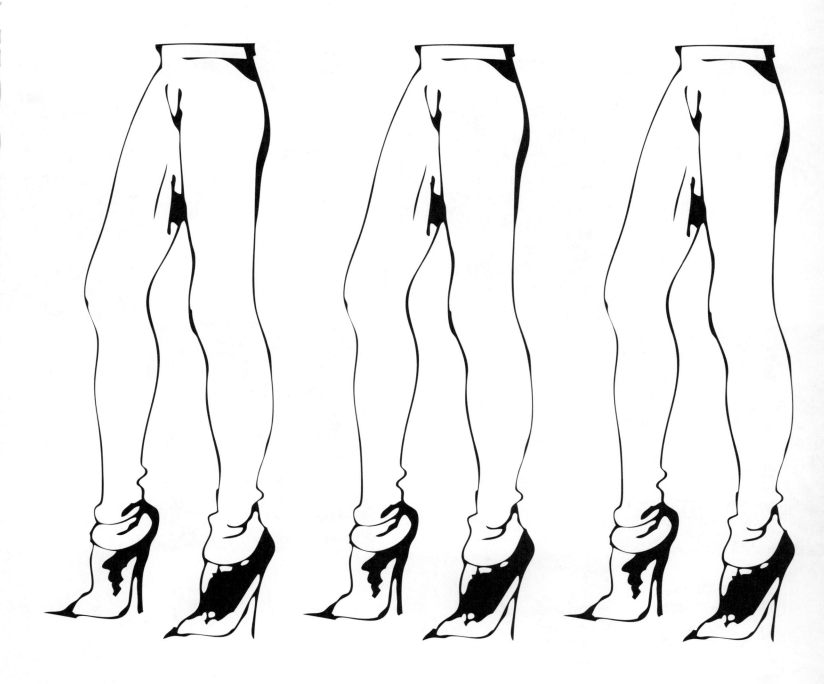

DESIGN YOUR LEGGINGS

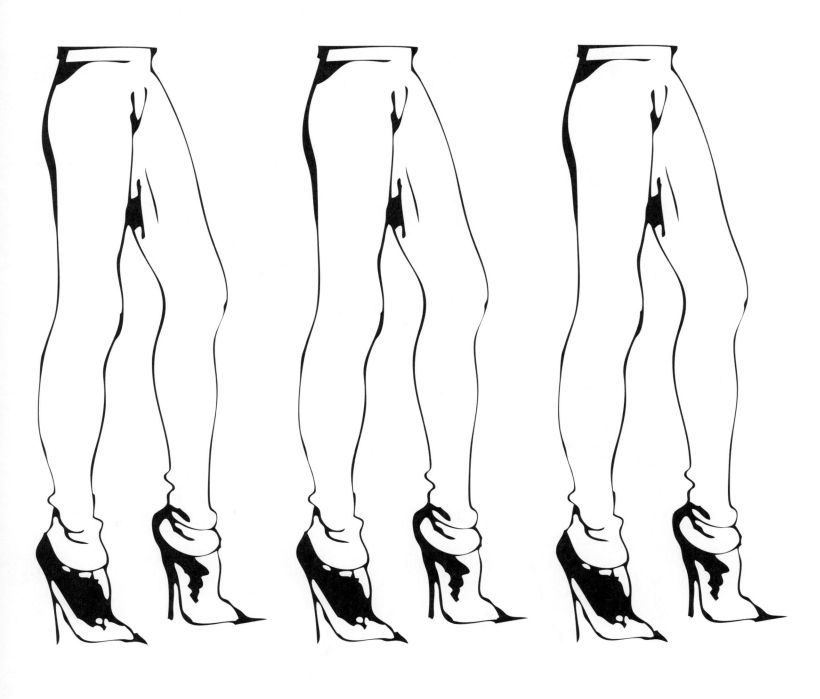

DESIGN YOUR LEGGINGS

COLOUR YOUR TIGHTS

DESIGN YOUR TIGHTS

SHOES SHOES SHOES

SHOES SHOES SHOES

# STOCKINGS & GARTERS

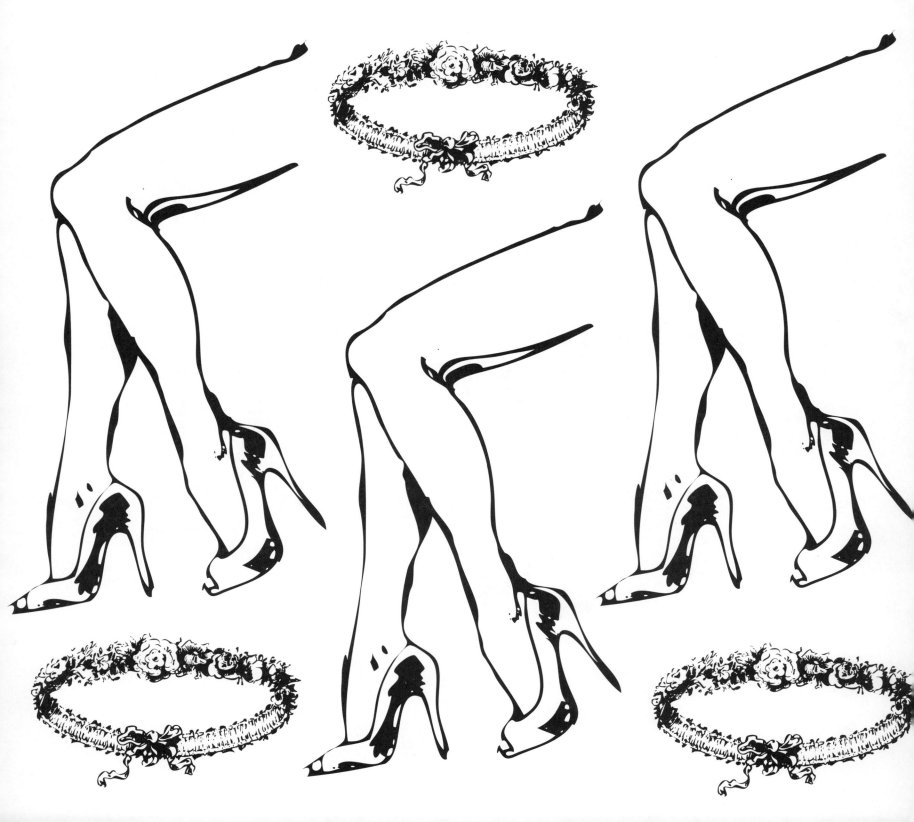

# STOCKINGS & GARTERS

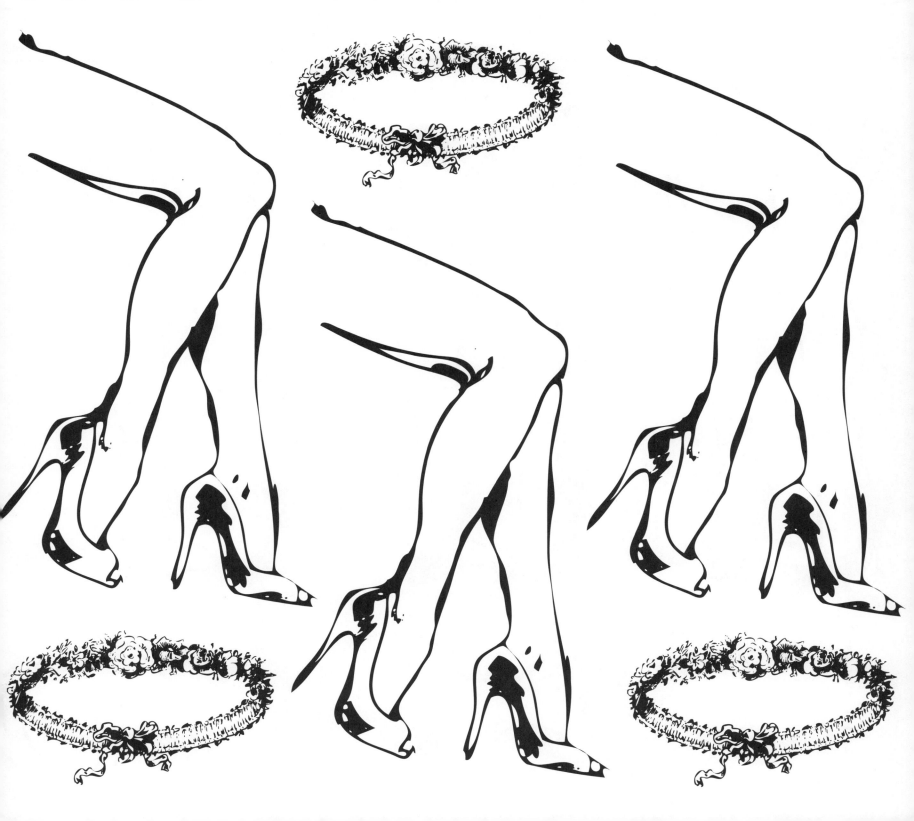

PINUP BODY STOCKING

PINUP UNDERWEAR

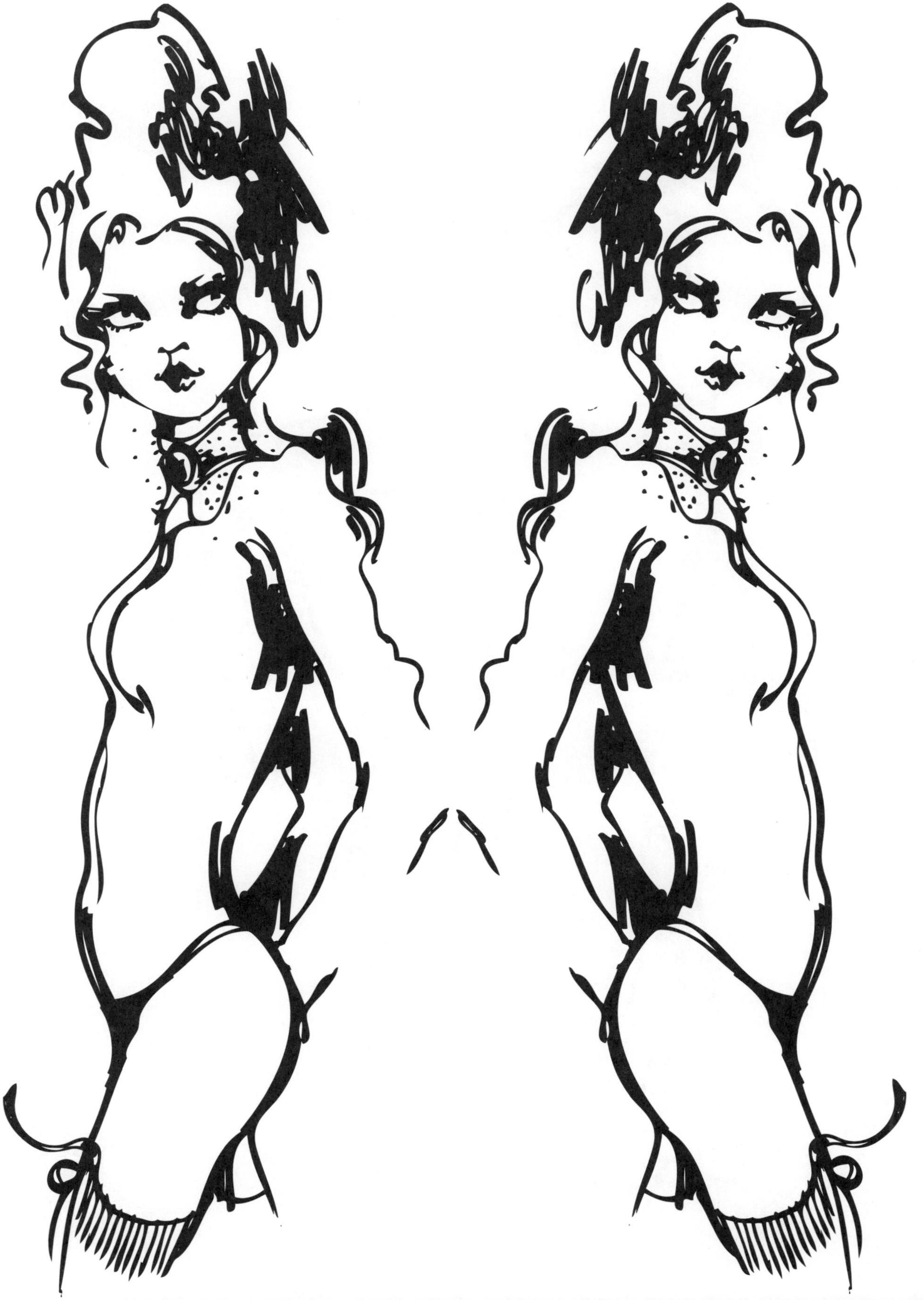

PINUP UNDERWEAR

FABRIC PRINT

ILLUSTRATION

YOUR OWN ILLUSTRATION

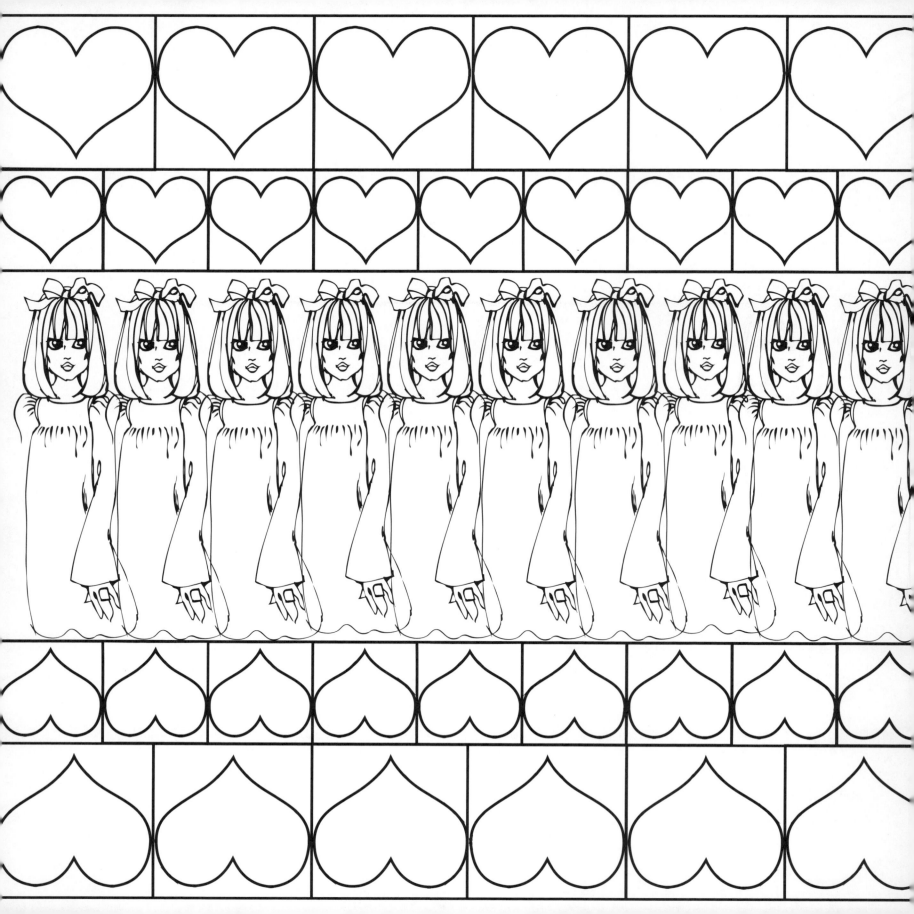

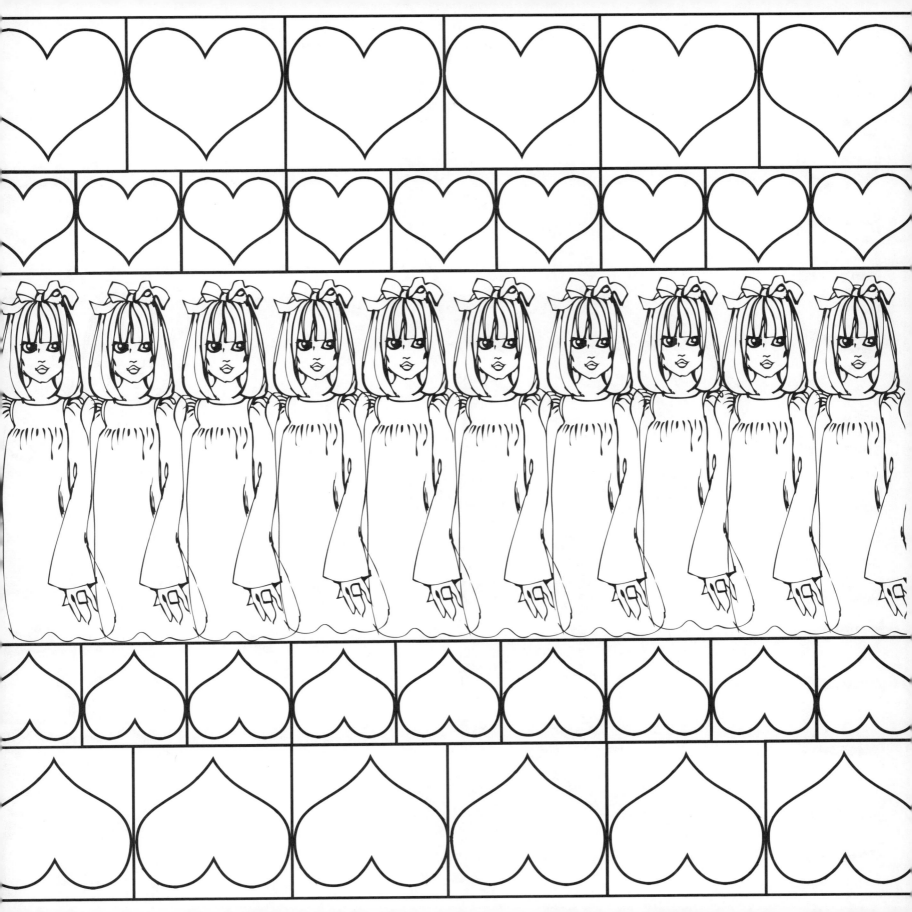

ILLUSTRATION

YOUR OWN ILLUSTRATION

ILLUSTRATION

YOUR OWN ILLUSTRATION

ILLUSTRATION

YOUR OWN ILLUSTRATION

ILLUSTRATION

YOUR OWN ILLUSTRATION

ILLUSTRATION

YOUR OWN ILLUSTRATION

ILLUSTRATION

YOUR OWN ILLUSTRATION

ILLUSTRATION

YOUR OWN ILLUSTRATION

ILLUSTRATION

YOUR OWN ILLUSTRATION

ILLUSTRATION

YOUR OWN ILLUSTRATION

YOUR OWN ILLUSTRATION

ILLUSTRATION

YOUR OWN ILLUSTRATION

ILLUSTRATION

YOUR OWN ILLUSTRATION

ILLUSTRATION

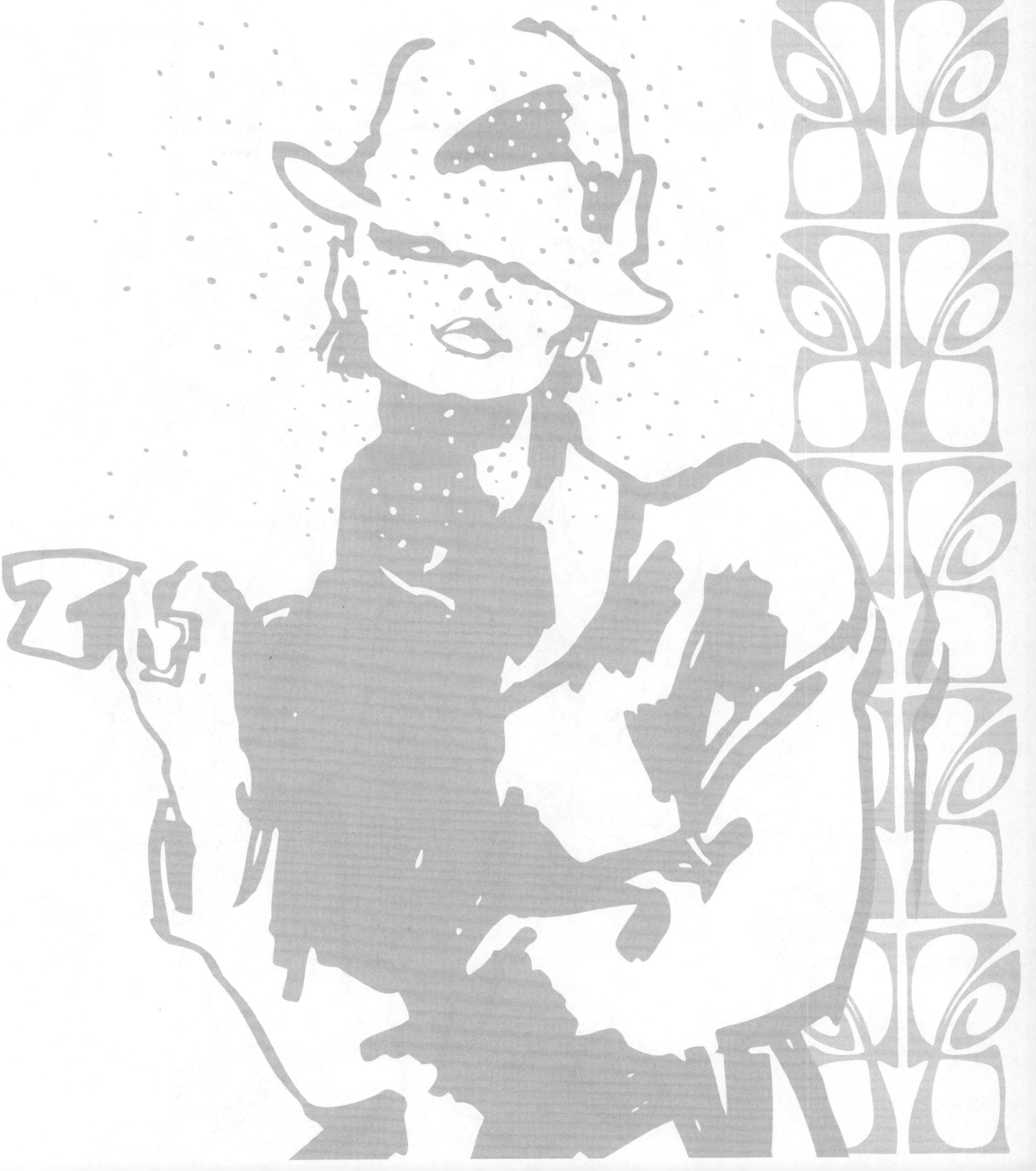

# ILLUSTRATION

# ILLUSTRATION

Many thanks to Mark Eastment, who as Publisher commissioned
THE BIBA YEARS whilst at the V&A and now this title. I would also like
to thank Felicity Price-Smith, Lauren Palma and Likrish Marchese.

Barbara Hulanicki, Miami

Published in 2016 by
Unicorn, an imprint of Unicorn Publishing Group LLP
101 Wardour Street
London
W1F OUG
www.unicornpublishing.org

ISBN 978-1-910787-34-2

10 9 8 7 6 5 4 3 2 1

Designed by Lauren Palma and Felicity Price-Smith
Printed in Spain by GraphyCems